AF454324

THE MOST ➤➤ FAMOUS

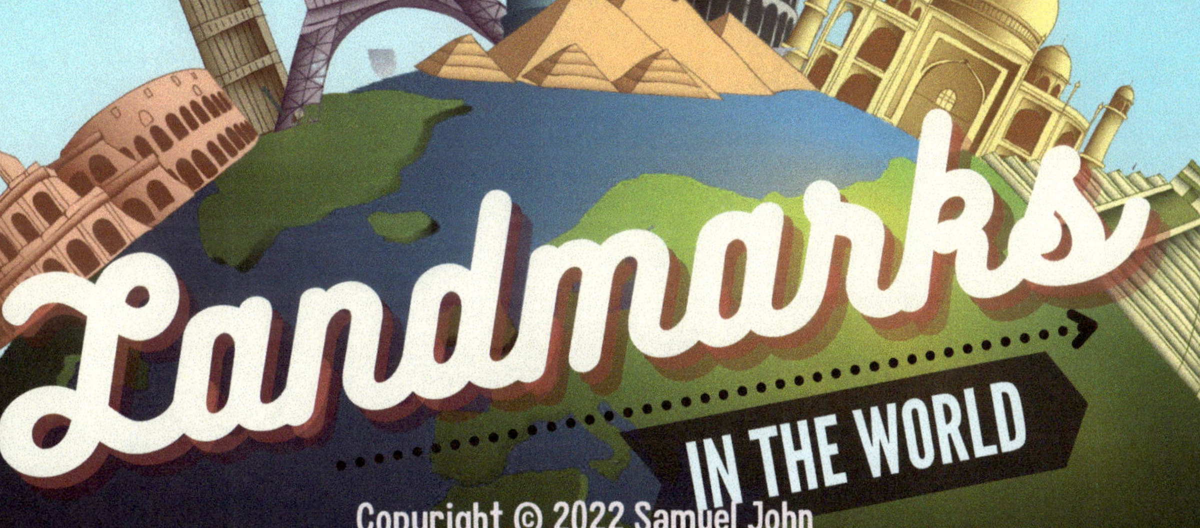

EIFFEL TOWER

Location: Paris, France.

- It was designed by Gustave Eiffel and built for the Universal Exhibition of 1889.

- It had to be dismantled later, but in the end they decided to preserve it.

- At first, people thought it was horrible.

- It is 324 meters high, has 1,665 steps, and is held together due to its 2.5 million screws.

- It is the fourth most visited monument in the world.

Taj Mahal

Location: Agra, India.

- It is a funerary monument built on the banks of the Yamuna River.

- Emperor Sha Jahan had it built in honor of his beloved wife, Mumtaz Mahal.

- Taj Mahal means "Crown Palace".

- It took 23 years to build it (1631–1654) and the work of more than 20,000 workers.

- It is one of the 7 Wonders of the Modern World.

GREAT WALL OF CHINA

Location: China.

- It was built in the 3rd century BC. by order of the emperor Qin.
- Its function was to prevent invaders from attacking from the north.
- Its total length is 21,196 km.
- It took about 2,000 years to build, going through several dynasties.
- Unlike popular belief, it cannot be seen from space.
- It is one of the 7 Wonders of the Modern World.

STATUE OF LIBERTY

Location: New York City, U.S.

- It was a <u>gift from France</u> to commemorate the centennial of the United States Declaration of Independence.

- <u>Represents</u> freedom opposite to oppression.

- The original name for the statue was Liberty enlightening the world.

- For several years it worked as a lighthouse.

- Its greenish color is due to the <u>oxidation</u> of the copper that covers the statue.

- Its height is 93 meters (or 305 feet), including the pedestal.

Sydney Opera House

Location: Sydney, Australia.

- It was designed by Danish architect Jørn Utzon, whose design was the winner in a competition in which 233 projects from 32 countries were submitted.

- They planned to spend 7 million dollars to build it, but it ended up costing 102 million Australian dollars.

- It measures 183 meters long, about 120 meters long, and 67 meters high.

- It was declared a World Heritage Site by UNESCO in 2007.

LINCOLN MEMORIAL

Location: Washington, D.C., U.S.

- It was built to honor the memory of President Abraham Lincoln.

- Inside the building, there is a statue of Lincoln looking towards the Washington Monument.

- It is one of the most visited monuments in the United States. It receives about 6 million tourists every year.

- There, Martin Luther King Jr. delivered his famous "I Have a Dream" speech.

NOTRE-DAME

Location: Paris, France.

- It is a cathedral dedicated to the Virgin Mary and one of the most famous monuments in Paris.
- "Notre Dame" <u>means</u> "Our Lady".
- It is located on the Ile de la Cité, in the middle of the Seine River.
- Victor Hugo placed Quasimodo, the hunchbacked character in his novel Our Lady of Paris, in Notre Dame.
- It is adorned with gargoyles, which serve to channel excess rainwater.

Colosseum

Location: Rome, Italy.

- The Romans enjoyed different shows In the Colosseum.

- It was originally called the Flavian Amphitheatre. But it was renamed the Colosseum after a nearby statue, the Colossus of Nero.

- It could accommodate 50,000 people.

- It was the largest amphitheatre built by the Roman Empire.

- It was inscribed on the UNESCO World Heritage List in 1980.

- ✅ It is one of the 7 Wonders of the Modern World.

MONT-SAINT-MICHEL

Location: Normandy, France.

- It is a <u>rocky islet</u> located in northwestern France, in the Normandy region.

- According to legend, the archangel Michael visited Bishop Aubert de Avranches in a dream, ordering him to build a church there.

- It was a prison during the French Revolution.

- It is one of the most visited tourist places in France, by more than 3 million tourists a year.

- It was declared a World Heritage Site by UNESCO in 1979.

PYRAMIDS OF GIZA

Location: Giza, Egypt.

- They are the most famous pyramids in Egypt.
- They are more than 4,000 years old.
- They were funerary temples. In them, the pharaohs were buried so that they could enjoy their life after death.
- The largest is Cheops. It is located next to those of Khafre and Menkaure.
- They are proof that the ancient Egyptians were great connoisseurs of mathematics and geometry.

GOLDEN GATE BRIDGE

Location: San Francisco, U.S.

- It is <u>the most recognized symbol</u> of San Francisco.
- Before it was built, people had to cross the strait by boat.
- It has the same name as the strait on which it is built.
- At the time of its construction, it was the <u>longest suspension bridge</u> in the world.
- It is 2.7 km long and 227 meters high.
- The bridge contains enough cable to circle the Earth three times.

CHRIST THE REDEEMER

Location: Rio de Janeiro, Brazil.

- It is also known as Christ of Corcovado. It is located on the top of Mount Corcovado, in the Tijuca National Park, at 710 meters above sea level.
- It is 38 meters high and weighs 1,145 tons.
- It was built in France and arrived in Brazil in pieces.
- In 2007 it was chosen as one of the 7 Wonders of the Modern World.

ACROPOLIS OF ATHENS

Location: Athens, Greece.

- The acropolises were enclosures that hosted important monuments and religious buildings, among others. The best known is the one in Athens.

- Contains 3 temples: the Parthenon, the Erechtheion, and the temple of Athena Nike.

- "Acropolis" means "high city". It is logical because they were in the highest areas of the cities.

- It was declared a World Heritage Site by UNESCO in 1987.

CHICHEN ITZA

Location: Mexico.

- It is a **complex of Mayan ruins** located in the **Yucatan** Peninsula.

- Chichén Itzá **means** "At the mouth of the well of the Itza ". Itza is the name of a Mayan people who lived in the Yucatan.

- Its main construction is the Pyramid of Kukulcán, also called "the Castle".

- In 1988 the whole area was declared a World Heritage Site by UNESCO.

- ✅ It is one of the 7 Wonders of the Modern World.

Kremlin

Location: Moscow, Russia.

- It is the headquarters of the Russian <u>government</u>. There are four palaces and four cathedrals inside its walled interior.

- It is located next to Red Square.

- "Kremlin" comes from the Russian word "kreml", which <u>means</u> "fortress inside a city".

- Its wall is about 2,500 meters long and is joined by a total of 20 towers.

- The Spásskaya Tower is the tallest and most impressive tower in the enclosure.

Big Ben

Location: London, United Kingdom.

- Big Ben is the name often used to refer to the clock tower located next to the Palace of Westminster. However, Big Ben is the name of the bell inside it.

- Elizabeth Tower is the actual name of the tower.

- Until 2012 its official name was Clock Tower.

- The awesome tower contains the largest four-faced clock in the world.

Petra

Location: Jordan.

- It is a city <u>carved into the rocks</u> and capital of the ancient Nabataean kingdom.

- Petra comes from the Greek word "Petros" and <u>means</u> "stone".

- It is known as "the Lost City". It was abandoned centuries ago, hidden under the sand, until the explorer Johann Ludwig Burckhardt rediscovered it in the 19th century.

- It has been the setting for movies such as Indiana Jones and the Last Crusade.

- It is one of the 7 Wonders of the Modern World.

Brandenburg Gate

Location: Berlin, Germany.

- It is an old gateway to Berlin. There were a total of twelve gates, and this is the only one that remains.
- Being a gateway, it was formerly on the edge of the city. It is currently located in the center.
- Until 1918 it could only be used by members of royalty and some privileged people.
- Its style is inspired by the Acropolis of Athens.

TEMPLES OF ANGKOR

Location: Angkor, Cambodia.

- They are <u>ancient stone temples</u> hidden in the middle of the jungle.

- Angkor Wat is the largest of all and the best preserved. <u>It</u> is considered <u>the largest religious construction in the world</u>.

- This temple appears on the Cambodian flag.

- There are about <u>1,000 temples</u> in the archaeological complex of Angkor.

- They were declared a World Heritage Site by UNESCO In 1992.

SAGRADA FAMILIA

Location: Barcelona, Spain.

- The Temple Expiatori de la Sagrada Família is a Catholic basilica designed by the architect Antoni Gaudí.

- It began in 1882, but today it is still under construction.

- It will be the tallest building in Barcelona and the tallest Christian church in the world when completed.

- It was declared a World Heritage Site by UNESCO in 2005.

DUOMO OF MILAN

Location: Milan, Italy.

- It is the cathedral of Milan.

- "Duomo" is an Italian word meaning "cathedral".

- It is one of the largest Catholic churches in the world.

- It is stated that it is decorated with 3,400 statues, 135 gargoyles, and another 700 figures.

- The highest point of the building is the Madonnina. It is a gilded copper statue that represents the Virgin.

TOWER OF PISA

Location: Pisa, Italy.

- Also known as the Leaning Tower of Pisa. It is the <u>bell tower</u> of the Duomo or cathedral of Pisa.

- Its construction began in 1773, and only 5 years later it <u>began to lean</u>.

- It is 8 floors high and has 294 steps.

- At first, it began to lean to the north. However, after completing the work on the bell tower, the tower began to lean to the south.

MOAI

Location: Easter Island, Chile.

- They are <u>gigantic stone statues</u> built by the natives of the island.

- "Moai" <u>means</u> "sculpture" in the Rapanui language.

- There are about 900 moai on the island.

- The Tukuturi moai is <u>the oldest</u> discovered.

- There are several theories regarding their meaning, but the most accepted defends that they are representations destined to worship the ancestors.

MOUNT RUSHMORE

Location: Keystone, U.S.

- Mount Rushmore National Memorial is a sculpture carved directly into the rock of a mountain.

- It represents the American presidents: George Washington, Thomas Jefferson, Theodore Roosevelt and Abraham Lincoln.

- The carved faces are 18 meters high.

- There is a secret vault called the "Hall of Records" behind the faces of the presidents.

And here it ends!

I hope you liked it and learned new things.

There are many more monuments and tourist places to discover: the Alhambra in Granada, the Basilica of Santa Sofía, Machu Picchu (which is another of the 7 Wonders of the Modern World)...

How many of these places did you know? Which ones have you visited? Which ones would you like to visit?

I want to ask you a favor so that this book reaches more people, and that is that you rate it with a sincere opinion on the platform where you purchased it.

With that small gesture, you will be helping me to carry on with new projects.

I can't wait to start creating my next book for you!

See you soon!

THE MOST
FAMOUS
Landmarks
IN THE WORLD

VOLCANOES
For Kids

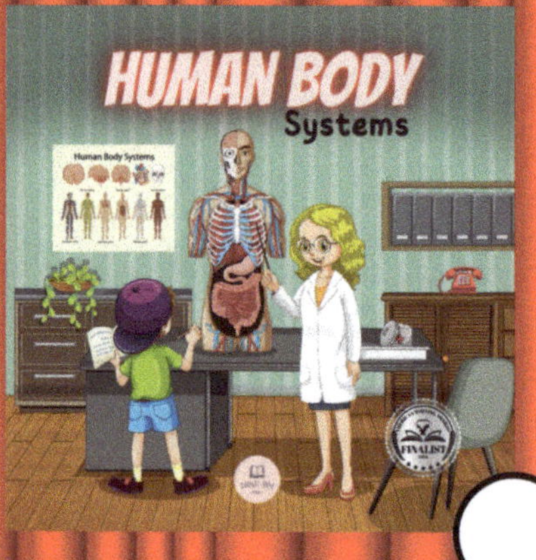

HUMAN BODY
Systems
Human Body Systems
FINALIST

FASCINATING
UNIVERSE
facts

DINOSAURS

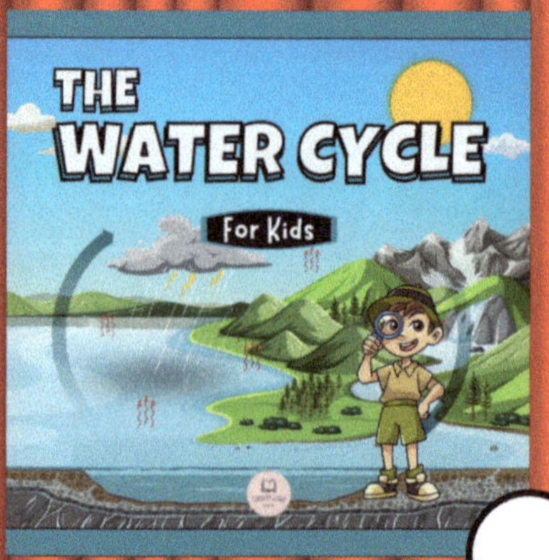

THE
WATER CYCLE
For Kids

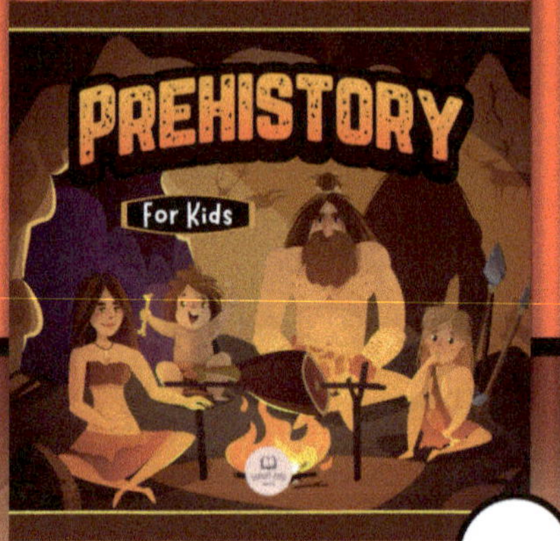

PREHISTORY
For Kids

ANCIENT
EGYPT

SCAN ME

I HAVE A GIFT FOR YOU!

This Free eBook is for You!

SCAN ME

https://www.bit.ly/samueljohngift

I HOPE YOU LIKE IT!

FOLLOW ME

www.amazon.com/author/samueljohnbooks

www.ingramcontent.com/pod-product-compliance
Lightning Source LLC
LaVergne TN
LVHW071943240726
843527LV00068B/346